NEW ZEALAND

EXPLORE THE COUNTRIES

Big Buddy Books

An Imprint of Abdo Publishing
www.abdopublishing.com

Julie Murray

www.abdopublishing.com

Published by Abdo Publishing, a division of ABDO, PO Box 398166, Minneapolis, Minnesota 55439.
Copyright © 2015 by Abdo Consulting Group, Inc. International copyrights reserved in all countries. No part
of this book may be reproduced in any form without written permission from the publisher. Big Buddy Books™
is a trademark and logo of Abdo Publishing.

Printed in the United States of America, North Mankato, Minnesota.
032014
092014

Cover Photo: Shutterstock.
Interior Photos: ASSOCIATED PRESS (pp. 15, 16, 17, 19, 23, 29, 31, 33), Glow Images (p. 35), iStockphoto
    (pp. 11, 25, 34), RoyalPress Nieboer/picture-alliance/dpa/AP Images (p. 13), Shutterstock (pp. 5, 9, 11, 19,
    21, 27, 34, 35, 37, 38).

Coordinating Series Editor: Rochelle Baltzer
Editor: Sarah Tieck
Contributing Editors: Bridget O'Brien, Marcia Zappa
Graphic Design: Adam Craven

Country population and area figures taken from the CIA World Factbook.

Library of Congress Cataloging-in-Publication Data

Murray, Julie, 1969-
 New Zealand / Julie Murray.
   pages cm. -- (Explore the countries)
 ISBN 978-1-62403-344-5
 1. New Zealand--Juvenile literature. I. Title.
 DU408.M87 2014
 993--dc23
                        2013046921

NEW ZEALAND

CONTENTS

AROUND THE WORLD

Our world has many countries. Each country has beautiful land. It has its own rich history. And, the people have their own languages and ways of life.

New Zealand is an island country. What do you know about New Zealand? Let's learn more about this place and its story!

Did You Know?

New Zealand has three official languages. These are English, Maori, and New Zealand Sign Language.

New Zealand is known for its snow-topped mountains and cloudy blue skies.

PASSPORT TO NEW ZEALAND

New Zealand is a group of islands in the Pacific Ocean. The two main islands are the North Island and the South Island. There are about 700 smaller islands.

New Zealand's total area is 103,363 square miles (267,710 sq km). More than 4.4 million people live there.

WHERE IN THE WORLD?

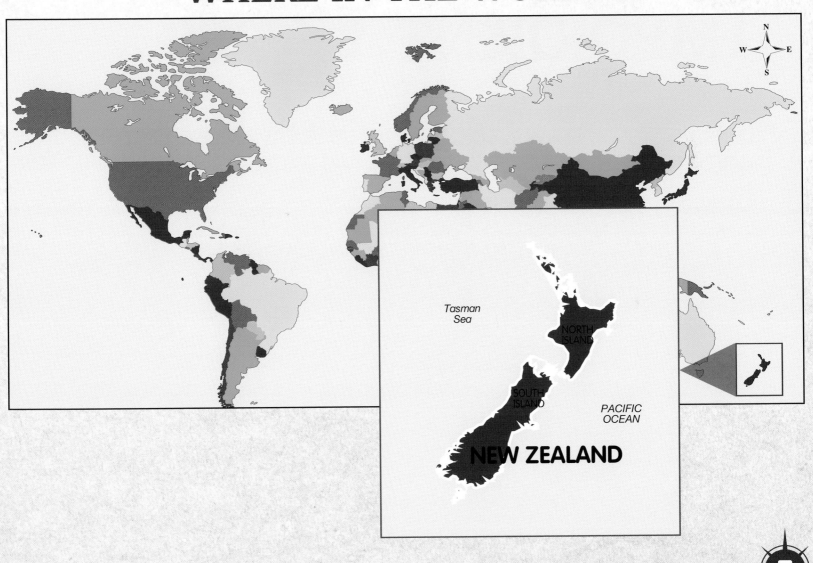

Tasman
Sea

NORTH
ISLAND

SOUTH
ISLAND

PACIFIC
OCEAN

NEW ZEALAND

IMPORTANT CITIES

Auckland is New Zealand's largest city. More than 400,000 people live there. Many more live in the smaller cities and towns around it.

Auckland is a leader in business. The city has two harbors. Many goods are shipped around the world from these busy ports.

8

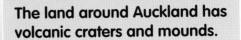

The land around Auckland has volcanic craters and mounds.

Boats dock at the Auckland Ferry Building.

Auckland

N
W E
S

Wellington

Christchurch

NEW ZEALAND

Christchurch is New Zealand's second-largest city. It is home to more than 348,000 people. Christchurch is on the Pacific Ocean. It is known for the arts. It has many parks.

Wellington is New Zealand's **capital** and one of its largest cities. Almost 180,000 people live there. Many more live in the cities and towns around it. It is the world's most southern capital.

The Avon River flows through Christchurch.

"The Beehive" is a well-known government building in Wellington.

NEW ZEALAND IN HISTORY

The first people known to live in New Zealand arrived around the 1200s. They are **ancestors** of the native Maori people. They settled the land.

In the 1600s and 1700s, Europeans began exploring the area. The first was Dutch sailor Abel Janszoon Tasman in 1642.

SAY IT
Maori
MAUR-ee

The Maori way of life is part of New Zealand's past and present. Today, Maori people sometimes perform dances.

Around 1770, British captain James Cook arrived. He mapped the islands. Soon, Europeans moved there to trade wood and animal goods. At first the Maori welcomed the trade. But over time, settlers took their land and changed their way of life.

In 1840, New Zealand became a British colony. In time, the colony gained more independence. In 1852, the Constitution Act created New Zealand's government. In 1947, New Zealand became a fully independent nation.

New Zealand soldiers fought alongside the British during World War II from 1939 to 1945.

New Zealand became a colony after the Treaty of Waitangi was signed in 1840. Today, events are held to honor Waitangi Day on February 6.

TIMELINE

1840

British officials signed the Treaty of Waitangi with more than 500 Maori rulers. This document gave ruling power to the Queen of England.

1777

James Cook printed his journal. It told Europeans about New Zealand's land and people.

1893

New Zealand became the first country to give women the right to vote.

1997

Jenny Shipley became New Zealand's first woman prime minister.

2011

A 6.3 **earthquake** hit Christchurch. More than 180 people were killed. The city and its people were still recovering from a 2010 earthquake.

1911

Native New Zealander Ernest Rutherford made an important theory in science. He came up with a model for how atoms are made up.

An Important Symbol

New Zealand's flag was adopted in 1902. It is blue, with a United Kingdom flag in the upper left corner. Four red stars are on the right side.

New Zealand's government is a **constitutional monarchy**. Parliament makes laws. The prime minister is the head of government. The king or queen of England is the head of state.

The flag's stars stand for the Southern Cross. This group of stars is seen at night in New Zealand.

Sir Jerry Mateparae (*right*) is the governor-general of New Zealand. He stands in for the queen of England.

ACROSS THE LAND

New Zealand is known for its beautiful land. There are fjords, beaches, mountains, farmland, **glaciers**, and forests. The North Island has **volcanoes**. The South Island is home to the Southern Alps.

New Zealand is bordered by the Pacific Ocean. It has lakes, waterfalls, and rivers. The country also has hot springs.

SAY IT

fjord
fee-AWRD

Did You Know?

In winter, New Zealand's average temperature is about 35°F (2°C) to 53°F (12°C). In summer, it is about 59°F (15°C) to 69°F (21°C).

Fjords are found on the country's coasts. These are deep, narrow bays of seawater.

New Zealand's highest peak is Mount Cook in the Southern Alps. It is 12,316 feet (3,754 m) high.

Many types of animals live in New Zealand. These include skinks, kiwis, red deer, frogs, and bats. Some of the country's animals are not found anywhere else in the world.

New Zealand is home to hundreds of different plants. These include evergreen and beech trees. Willows, poplars, and gorse also grow there.

Did You Know?

Sometimes people use "kiwi" as a nickname for a New Zealander.

Kiwi birds only live in New Zealand. They cannot fly.

EARNING A LIVING

In New Zealand, most people have service jobs. They work for places such as banks, schools, and hotels. The country's factories make forest and farm products to sell around the world.

New Zealand has many **natural resources**. Fish and oysters come from its waters. Farmers produce apples, barley, kiwi fruit, and grapes. They raise cattle and sheep.

Did You Know?

Gold is an important product of New Zealand.

Sheep and cattle live on farms in New Zealand's countryside. They provide meat, wool, and dairy products.

LIFE IN NEW ZEALAND

Most New Zealanders live in modern cities. Others live in the country's **rural** areas. They raise sheep or cattle or grow crops.

Beef and seafood are popular foods in New Zealand. People there also enjoy dairy foods such as ice cream, milk, and cheese. They drink tea, coffee, beer, and wine.

Meat pies (*above*) are a popular handheld food. A favorite dessert is pavlova (*right*).

Did You Know?

In New Zealand, children must attend school from ages 6 to 16.

New Zealanders enjoy sports. People watch and play rugby football. It is considered the national sport. They also like cricket.

New Zealand has beautiful land for outdoor activities and sports. Many people enjoy mountain climbing, hiking, boating, and surfing. People also fish and hunt.

The All Blacks is the country's national rugby football team. They do a Maori dance before playing.

FAMOUS FACES

Sir Edmund Hillary was a famous mountain climber. He was born in Auckland on July 20, 1919.

In 1953, Hillary became one of the first people to climb Mount Everest. Many people had tried and failed to do this. Hillary went on to climb more mountains. He wrote books about his adventures. He died in 2008.

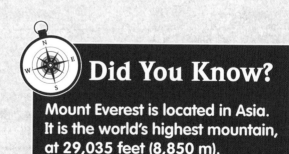

Did You Know?

Mount Everest is located in Asia. It is the world's highest mountain, at 29,035 feet (8,850 m).

Hillary (*left*) climbed Mount Everest with Tenzing Norgay (*right*).

Sir Peter Jackson is known for his film work. He was born on October 31, 1961, in Pukerua Bay, North Island. He first started making movies at age eight, when his parents bought him a camera.

Jackson is famous for his Lord of the Rings movies. They are based on J.R.R. Tolkien's books of the same name. He also directed movies based on Tolkien's *The Hobbit*. The first two came out in 2012 and 2013.

Did You Know?

Jackson filmed all three Lord of the Rings movies in New Zealand. It took about 15 months.

Jackson's Lord of the Rings movies won 17 Oscars.

TOUR BOOK

Imagine traveling to New Zealand! Here are some places you could go and things you could do.

Learn

Spend some time at Te Papa Tongarewa in Wellington. It is the country's national museum. There, you can learn about the history and art of New Zealand.

Ride

Wellington has a popular cable car system. You can ride from the business district to the botanic gardens.

 ## Play

Spend time at Ninety Mile Beach on the North Island. You can watch the sunset, build a sand castle, or go bodyboarding!

Explore

Walk through Kelly Tarlton's SEA LIFE Aquarium in Auckland. You'll see penguins, sharks, and stingrays!

 ## See

Visit Sutherland Falls on the South Island. It is the fifth-highest mountain waterfall in the world. Some say the falling water sounds as loud as an airplane taking off!

A Great Country

The story of New Zealand is important to our world. New Zealand is a land of beautiful mountains and coasts. It is a country built by native Maori people and settlers.

The people and places that make up this country offer something special. They help make the world a more interesting place.

Wanaka Lake is known for its beauty.
This area is popular with visitors.

New Zealand Up Close

Official Name: New Zealand

Flag:

Population (rank): 4,401,916
(July 2014 est.)
(127th most-populated country)

Total Area (rank): 103,363 square miles
(76th largest country)

Capital: Wellington

Official Language: English, Maori, New Zealand Sign Language

Currency: New Zealand dollar

Form of Government: Constitutional monarchy

National Anthem: "God Defend New Zealand"

Important Words

ancestor a family member from an earlier time.

capital a city where government leaders meet.

constitutional monarchy (kahnt-stuh-TOO-shnuhl MAH-nuhr-kee) a form of government in which a king or queen has only those powers given by a country's laws and constitution.

earthquake (UHRTH-kwayk) a shaking of a part of the earth.

glacier (GLAY-shuhr) a huge chunk of ice and snow on land.

natural resources useful and valued supplies from nature.

rural of or relating to open land away from towns and cities.

volcano a deep opening in Earth's surface from which hot liquid rock or steam comes out.

Websites

To learn more about Explore the Countries, visit **booklinks.abdopublishing.com**. These links are routinely monitored and updated to provide the most current information available.

INDEX